Crozier Surname

Ireland: 1600s to 1900s

From Ireland Church Records of Baptism, Marriage and Death

Comprised of Roman Catholic and Church of Ireland Records

From Counties Carlow, Cork, Kerry and Dublin City

Compiled by **Donovan Hurst**

February 20, 2013

ISBN: 1939958008
ISBN-13: 978-1-939958-00-6

Dedication

This work is dedicated to all of those that came before us and shaped
our lives to make us the people that we are today.

Table of Contents

Introduction

This is a compilation of individuals who have the surname of Crozier that lived in the country of Ireland from the 1600s to the 1900s. I have placed each entry into one of four categories: Families, Individual Births/Baptisms, Individual Burials, and Individual Marriages. If a marriage entry primarily concerns an Individual Crozier whom is female, then I have placed that entry under the category of Individual Marriages. If a marriage entry primarily concerns an Individual Crozier whom is male, then I have placed that entry under the category of Families. Images of many of these listings are available at http://churchrecords.irishgenealogy.ie/churchrecords/.

To help guide the reader of this work, the format of this book is as follows:

- Main Family Entry (Husband and Wife) (Father and Mother)

   o Child of Main Family Entry, including Spouse(s) when available

      ▪ Grandchild of Main Family Entry, including Spouse(s) when available

         • Great-Grandchild of Main Family Entry, including Spouse(s) when available

(**Bolded Text**) following any entry includes any additional information such as Residence(s), Occupation(s), Signature(s), etc. when available.

Hurst

Some of the fonts used in this work symbolizes Celtic writing. The traditional letters, numbers, and punctuation marks and their Celtic counterparts are as follows:

Traditional Letters (Uppercase & Lowercase)

A a B b C c D d E f G g H h I i J j K k L l M m N n O o P p Q q R r S s T t U u V v W w X x Y y Z z

Celtic Letters (Uppercase & Lowercase)

A a B b C c D ð E e F f G g H h I i J j K k L l M m

N n O o P p Q q R r S s T t U u V v W w X x Y y Z z

Traditional Numbers

1 2 3 4 5 6 7 8 9 10

Celtic Numbers

1 2 3 4 5 6 7 8 9 10

Traditional Punctuation

. , : ' " & - ( )

Celtic Punctuation

. , : ' " & - ( )

Crozier Surname Ireland: 1600s to 1900s

Parish Churches

Carlow (Church of Ireland)

Carlow Parish.

Cork & Ross

(Roman Catholic or RC)

Bantry Parish and Courcy's Country or Ballinspittal Parish.

Dublin (Church of Ireland)

Arbour Hill Barracks Parish, Irishtown Parish, North Strand Parish, Rathmines Parish, Sandford Parish, St. Andrew Parish, St. Anne Parish, St. Audoen Parish, St. George Parish, St. James Parish, St. Mark Parish, St. Mary Parish, St. Nicholas Without Parish, St. Paul Parish, St. Peter Parish, St. Stephen Parish, and Taney Parish.

Dublin (Roman Catholic or RC)

Rathfarnham Parish, SS. Michael & John Parish, St. Agatha Parish, St. Andrew Parish, St. Audoen Parish, St. Lawrence Parish, St. Mary Parish, St. Mary, Donnybrook Parish, St. Mary, Pro Cathedral Parish, St. Michan Parish, and St. Nicholas Parish.

Kerry (Church of Ireland)

Aghadoe Parish, Castleisland Parish, and Tralee Parish.

Kerry (Roman Catholic or RC)

Tralee Parish.

⒡amilies

- Andrew Crozier & Margaret Potts – 3 Jan 1853 (Marriage, **St. Mary Parish (RC)**)

  o Margaret Mary Crozier – b. 1858, bapt. 1858 (Baptism, **St. Andrew Parish (RC)**)

  o Thomas Andrew Crozier – b. 1863, bapt. 1863 (Baptism, **St. Andrew Parish (RC)**)

Andrew Crozier (father):

Residence - Lower Pembroke Street - 1858

1 Windsor Place - 1863

Wedding Witnesses:

Christopher Cusack & M. A. Crozier

- Andrew Crozier & Unknown

Signature:

Hurst

- ○ Margaret Crozier & Matthew Thornicroft (T h o r n i c r o f t) – 1 Jun 1879 (Marriage, **St. Andrew Parish**)

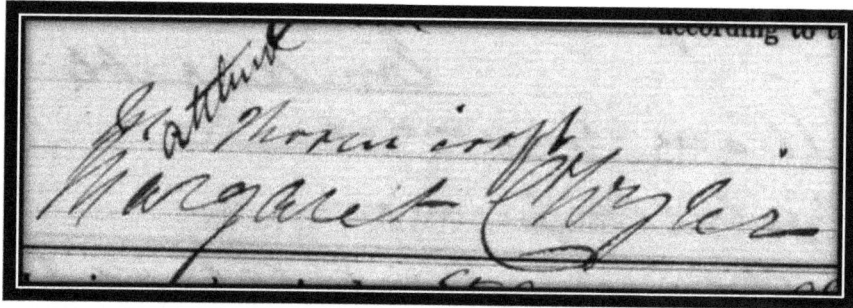

Signatures:

Margaret Crozier (daughter):

    Residence - 65 Dame Street - June 1, 1879

    Relationship Status at Marriage - minor

Matthew Thornicroft, son of Thomas Thornicroft (son-in-law):

    Residence - 24 Upper Sheriff Street - June 1, 1879

    Occupation - Mechanical Engineer - June 1, 1879

Thomas Thornicroft (father):

    Occupation - Farmer

Andrew Crozier (father):

    Occupation - House Painter

Crozier Surname Ireland: 1600s to 1900s

Wedding Witnesses:

Andrew Crozier & Deborah Haskins

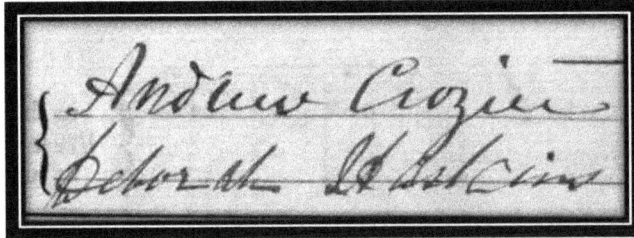

Signatures:

- Arthur Crozier & Elizabeth Crozier

  o John Crozier – bapt. 28 Jun 1818 (Baptism, **St. Paul Parish**)

- Christopher Crozier & Anne Crozier

  o Frederick Crozier – b. 4 Mar 1865, bapt. 30 Apr 1865 (Baptism, **Arbour Hill Barracks Parish**)

  o John James Crozier – bapt. 30 Apr 1865 (Baptism, **Arbour Hill Barracks Parish**)

Christopher Crozier (father):

Residence - Royal Barracks - April 30, 1865

Occupation - Private, 61st Regiment - April 30, 1865

- George Crozier, b. 1816, bur. 19 Aug 1872 (Burial, **St. George Parish**) & Emily Anne Foster

  o Helen Jane Crozier – b. 14 Apr 1860, bapt. 10 May 1860 (Baptism, **St. Peter Parish**)

  o Emily Constance Crozier, b. 6 Feb 1862, bapt. 28 Mar 1862 (Baptism, **St. Peter Parish**) & Edward Dillon – 16 Oct 1885 (Marriage, **St. George Parish**)

Hurst

Signatures:

Emily Constance Crozier (daughter):

    Residence - 9 Upper Temple Street - October 16, 1885

Edward Dillon, son of Charles Dillon (son-in-law):

    Residence - 47 Upper Leeson Street - October 16, 1885

    Occupation - Merchant - October 16, 1885

Charles Dillon (father):

    Occupation - Solicitor

George Crozier (father):

    Occupation - Solicitor

Wedding Witnesses:

James MacGregor Millar & Alfred Fitz Clarence Crozier

Signatures:

Crozier Surname Ireland: 1600s to 1900s

- William George Crozier – b. 25 Oct 1863, bapt. 18 Dec 1863 (Baptism, **St. Peter Parish**), bur. 8 Mar 1873 (Burial, **St. George Parish**)

William George Crozier (son):

Residence - 9 Upper Temple Street - before March 8, 1873

Age at Death - 9 years

- Alfred Fitz Clarence Crosier – b. 19 Aug 1865, bapt. 5 Oct 1865 (Baptism, **St. Peter Parish**), bur. 1 Nov 1890 (Burial, **St. George Parish**)

Signature:

Alfred Fitz Clarence Crozier (son):

Residence - 9 Temple Street - before November 1, 1890

Age at Death - 25 years

- Edward Travers Crozier – b. 10 Jun 1867, bapt. 11 Jul 1867 (Baptism, **St. Peter Parish**)

George Crozier (father):

Residence - 24 York Street - May 10, 1860

March 28, 1862

December 18, 1863

October 5, 1865

July 11, 1867

Hurst

9 Upper Temple Street - before August 19, 1872

Occupation - Solicitor - May 10, 1860

March 28, 1862

December 18, 1863

October 5, 1865

July 11, 1867

Age at Death - 56 years

Remarks about Burial - paid for on October 5, 1872

- George Crozier & Mary Crozier
  - Anne Mary Crozier – bapt. 16 Jun 1808 (Baptism, St. Mary Parish)
- George Crozier & Unknown
  - Elizabeth Florence Crozier & Thomas James MacDonagh – 6 Aug 1900 (Marriage, St. Anne Parish)

Signatures:

Elizabeth Florence Crozier (daughter):

Residence - Water Street, Enniskillen - August 6, 1900

Thomas James MacDonagh, son of Thomas MacDonagh (son-in-law):

Residence - 91 Grafton Street - August 6, 1900

Occupation - Book Keeper - August 6, 1900

Thomas MacDonagh (father):

Occupation - Postmaster

George Crozier (father):

Occupation - Coachbuilder

Wedding Witnesses:

David John Rea & Charlotte Anne McDonnell

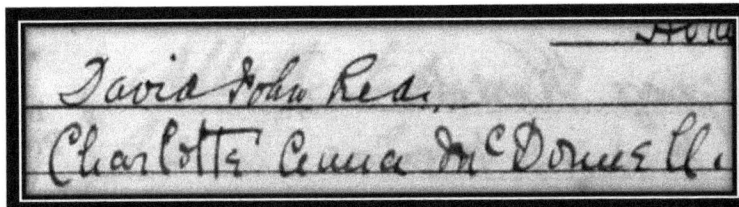

Signatures:

- Gulielmo Crozier & Catherine Coleman
  - Margaret Crozier & Patrick Hawkins – 7 Aug 1859 (Marriage, **St. Nicholas Parish (RC)**)
    - Mary Teresa Hawkins – b. 27 Jan 1862, bapt. 29 Jan 1862 (Baptism, **St. Nicholas Parish (RC)**)

Margaret Crozier (daughter):

Residence - 5 Montague Court - August 7, 1859

Patrick Hawkins, son of Patrick Hawkins & Catherine Unknown (son-in-law):

Residence - 5 Montague Court - August 7, 1859

January 29, 1862

Wedding Witnesses:

Edward Sherwood & Patrick Hickey

- Henderson Crozier & Unknown

  o Mary Crozier (1st Marriage) & Unknown Bell

  o Mary Crozier Bell (2nd Marriage) & Thomas George Rowland – 26 Feb 1859 (Marriage, St. George Parish)

Signatures:

Mary Crozier Bell (daughter):

Residence - Christianstown, Co. Louth - February 26, 1859

Relationship Status at Marriage - widow

Thomas George Rowland, son of John Rowland (son-in-law):

Residence - 1 Hardwicke Street - February 26, 1859

White Mills, Co. Louth - February 26, 1859

Occupation - Corn Merchant - February 26, 1859

John Rowland (father):

Occupation - Esquire

Henderson Crozier (father):

Occupation - Esquire

Wedding Witnesses:

William Whitton & John Thomas Rowland

Signatures:

- Henry Crozier & Bridget Unknown

  o Bridget Crozier & Patrick McCabe – 15 Aug 1869 (Marriage, **St. Andrew Parish** (RC))

Bridget Crozier (daughter):

Residence - 68 Lower Baggot Street - August 15, 1869

Patrick McCabe, son of Lawrence McCabe & Catherine Unknown (son-in-law):

Residence - Rathmines - August 15, 1869

Wedding Witnesses:

Lawrence McCabe & Jane Free

- James Crozier & Emma Unknown

  o Emma Charlotte Crozier – b. 7 May 1849, bapt. 22 Sep 1850 (Baptism, **St. James Parish**)

  o Harriet Maude Crozier – b. 1 Sep 1850, bapt. 22 Sep 1850 (Baptism, **St. James Parish**)

  o George Frederick Crozier – b. 16 Apr 1852, bapt. 9 May 1852 (Baptism, **St. Peter Parish**)

  o Kathleen Elizabeth Crozier – b. 7 Nov 1853, bapt. 19 Mar 1854 (Baptism, **St. Peter Parish**)

  o Edward William Crozier – b. 2 Jan 1855, bapt. 14 Jan 1855 (Baptism, **St. Peter Parish**)

James Crozier (father):

Residence - Island Bridge Barrack - September 22, 1850

Portobello Barracks - May 9, 1852

March 19, 1854

Hurst

7 Clanbrassil Place - January 14, 1855

Occupation - Mess Master - September 22, 1850

May 9, 1852

March 19, 1854

January 14, 1855

- James Crozier & Julie Byrne (B y r n e)

  - Julie Mary Crosier – b. 22 Apr 1871, bapt. 12 May 1871 (Baptism, **St. Agatha Parish** (RC))

James Crozier (father):

Residence - 4 Portland Row West - May 12, 1871

- John Crozier & Amelia Kelly – 26 Jan 1827 (Marriage, **St. Andrew Parish** (RC))

  - Mary Jane Crozier – bapt. 1827 (Baptism, **St. Andrew Parish** (RC))

  - Mary Crozier – bapt. 1831 (Baptism, **St. Andrew Parish** (RC))

  - Amelia Crozier – bapt. 1835 (Baptism, **St. Mary Parish** (RC))

  - John Crozier – bapt. 1837 (Baptism, **St. Mary Parish** (RC))

  - James Crozier – bapt. 1839 (Baptism, **St. Mary Parish** (RC))

- John Crozier & Emma Unknown

  - Robert Crozier – bapt. 1829 (Baptism, **St. Andrew Parish** (RC))

  - Anne Crozier – bapt. 1833 (Baptism, **St. Andrew Parish** (RC))

  - Elizabeth Crozier – bapt. 1841 (Baptism, **St. Andrew Parish** (RC))

  - Christine Crozier – bapt. 1846 (Baptism, **St. Andrew Parish** (RC))

- John Crozier & Frances Catherine Bailey – 5 Jun 1820 (Marriage, **St. Peter Parish**)

Crozier Surname Ireland: 1600s to 1900s

John Crozier (husband):

Residence - Gorta, Co. Fermangh - June 5, 1820

Frances Catherine Bailey (wife):

Residence - St. Peter Parish - June 5, 1820

Wedding Witnesses:

Thomas Bailey & Richard Conolly

- John Crozier & Mary Comber – 16 Sep 1791 (Marriage, **St. Paul Parish**)
- John Crozier & Mary Crozier, bur. 31 Aug 1827 (Burial, **St. Mary Parish**)
  - Robert Crozier – bapt. 13 Mar 1785 (Baptism, **St. Mary Parish**)
  - William Crozier – bapt. 28 May 1786 (Baptism, **St. Mary Parish**)
  - James Crozier – bapt. 5 Dec 1788 (Baptism, **St. Mary Parish**)
  - Mary Crozier – bapt. 14 Jun 1791 (Burial, **St. Mary Parish**)
  - Unknown (Child) – bur. 18 Jun 1793 (Burial, **St. Mary Parish**)

Unknown (Child):

Residence - Cole's Lane - before June 18, 1793

  - James Crozier – bapt. 8 Mar 1795 (Burial, **St. Mary Parish**)

John Crozier (father):

Residence - Cole's Lane - December 5, 1788

June 14, 1791

March 8, 1795

Hurst

Mary Crozier (mother):

Residence - Cole's Lane - before August 31, 1827

- John Crozier & Mary Crozier
  - William Crozier – bapt. 8 Oct 1795 (Baptism, **Carlow Parish**)

John Crozier (father):

Residence - Galway - October 8, 1795

- John Crozier & Mary Crozier
  - Joseph Crozier – bapt. 12 Dec 1813 (Baptism, **St. Mary Parish**)
- John Crozier & Mary Murphy – 9 Feb 1823 (Marriage, **St. Mary, Pro Cathedral Parish (RC)**)
- John Crozier & Mary Unknown
  - Frances Crozier – bapt. 1824 (Baptism, **St. Andrew Parish (RC)**)
  - John Crozier – bapt. 1825 (Baptism, **St. Andrew Parish (RC)**)
- John Crozier & Mary Anne Brough – 13 Sep 1859 (Marriage, **St. Mary Parish (RC)**)
  - John Josh Crozier – bapt. 1860 (Baptism, **St. Mary Parish (RC)**)
  - Anne Elizabeth Crozier – b. 1862, bapt. 1862 (Baptism, **Rathfarnham Parish (RC)**)
  - William James Crozier – b. 1863, bapt. 1863 (Baptism, **St. Andrew Parish (RC)**)

John Crozier (father):

Residence - Roundtown - 1862

55 Mount Street - 1863

Crozier Surname Ireland: 1600s to 1900s

- John Crozier & Unknown

  o Baptist Barton Crozier & Catherine Mary Bolland – 25 Feb 1851 (Marriage, **St. George Parish**)

Signatures:

Baptist Barton Crozier (son):

    Residence - 70 Eccles Street - February 25, 1851

    Occupation - Clergyman - February 25, 1851

Catherine Mary Bolland, daughter of John Bolland (daughter-in-law):

    Residence - 46 Upper Rutland Street - February 25, 1851

John Bolland (father):

    Occupation - Esquire

John Crozier (father):

    Occupation - Esquire

Wedding Witnesses:

Joseph Bolland & John Crozier

Signatures:

Hurst

○ Jane Crozier & William Nicholson – 15 Sep 1853 (Marriage, St. George Parish)

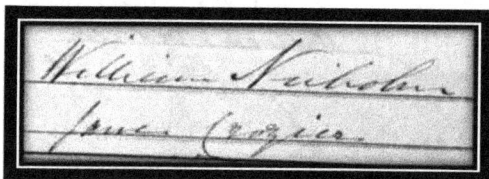

Signatures:

Jane Crozier (daughter):

    Residence - Nelson Street - September 15, 1853

William Nicholson, son of John Nicholson (son-in-law):

    Residence - Mohill, Co. Letrim - September 15, 1853

    Occupation - Writing Clerk - September 15, 1853

John Nicholson (father):

    Occupation - Farmer

John Crozier (father):

    Occupation - Esquire

Wedding Witnesses:

Thomas Charles Crozier & William Flaherty

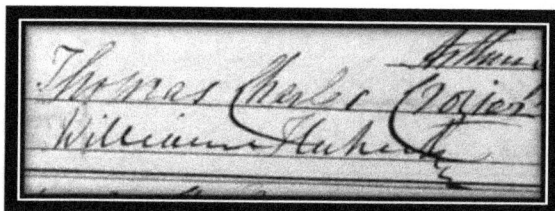

Signatures:

14

Crozier Surname Ireland: 1600s to 1900s

o John Crozier & Anne Tymons – 30 Apr 1861 (Marriage, **St. George Parish**)

Signatures:

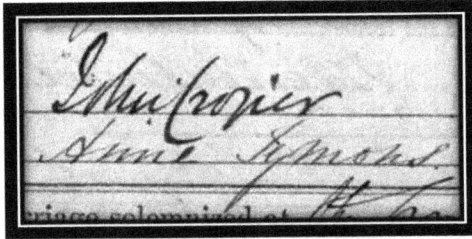

- John George Crozier, b. 22 Apr 1869, bapt. 12 May 1869 (Baptism, **St. George Parish**) & Georgina Marian Unknown
  - John Spencer Noel Crozier – b. 6 Jan 1896, bapt. 14 Feb 1896 (Baptism, **St. Stephen Parish**)

John George Crozier (son):

Residence - Gortia House, Co. Fermangh - February 14, 1896

Occupation - Jeweler - February 14, 1896

John Crozier (son):

Residence - 66 Lower Leeson Street, St. Peter Parish - April 30, 1861

Gortra, Co. Fermangh - May 12, 1869

Occupation - Esquire - April 30, 1861

Esquire, J P [Justice of the Peace] **- May 12, 1869**

Anne Tymons, daughter of James Tymons (daughter-in-law):

Residence - 14 Gardiner's Place - April 30, 1861

James Tymons (father):

Occupation - Esquire

Hurst

John Crozier (father):

   Occupation - Esquire

Wedding Witnesses:

James Tymons & George Mansfield

Signatures:

     o   Frances Crozier & Alexander Eccles Auchinleck – 3 Jun 1862 (Marriage, **St. Peter Parish**)

Signatures:

Frances Crozier (daughter):

   Residence - 66 Lower Leeson Street - June 3, 1862

Alexander Eccles Auchinleck, son of James E. Auchinleck (son-in-law):

   Residence - Rye, Sussex - June 3, 1862

   Occupation - Clerk in Holy Orders - June 3, 1862

James E. Auchinleck (father):

   Occupation - Clerk in Holy Orders

Crozier Surname Ireland: 1600s to 1900s

John Crozier (father):

Occupation - **J P** [Justice of the Peace]

Wedding Witnesses:

John Andrew & John Crozier

Signatures:

○ Catherine Crozier & Benjamin Armstrong – 2 Mar 1864 (Marriage, **St. Peter Parish**)

Signatures:

Catherine Crozier (daughter):

Residence - **66 Lower Leeson Street** - March 2, 1864

Benjamin Armstrong, son of Joseph Armstrong (son-in-law):

Residence - **Woodfort, Enniskeen Parish, Co. Meath** - March 2, 1864

Occupation - **Esquire** - March 2, 1864

Relationship Status at Marriage - **widow**

Hurst

Joseph Armstrong (father):

    Occupation - Esquire

John Crozier (father):

    Occupation - Esquire

Wedding Witnesses:

Thomas M. Moore & Mark Moore

Signatures:

- John Crozier & Unknown
  - Mary Anne Crozier & Thomas Whitley – 3 Jan 1853 (Marriage, **St. Mark Parish**)

Signatures:

Crozier Surname Ireland: 1600s to 1900s

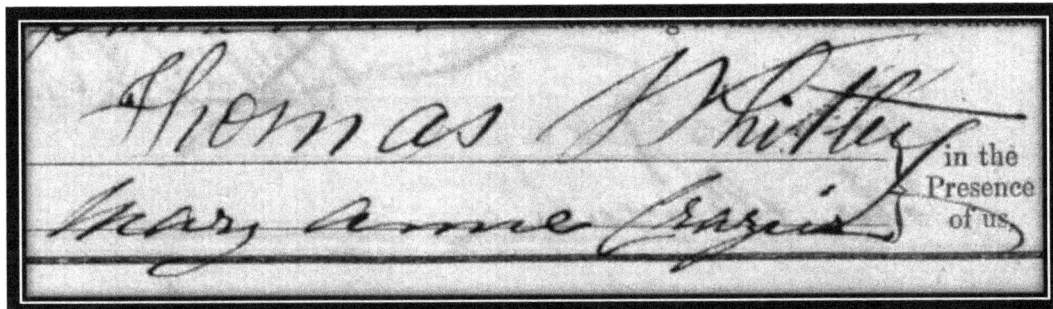

Mary Anne Crozier (daughter):

    Residence - 2 Shaw Villa, St. Mark Parish - January 3, 1853

Thomas Whitley, son of James Whitley (son-in-law):

    Residence - 2 Shaw Villa, St. Mark Parish - January 3, 1853

    Occupation - Tailor - January 3, 1853

    Relationship Status at Marriage - widow

James Whitley (father):

    Occupation - Farmer

Wedding Witnesses:

Jeremiah Maguire & John Guilfoyle

Signatures:

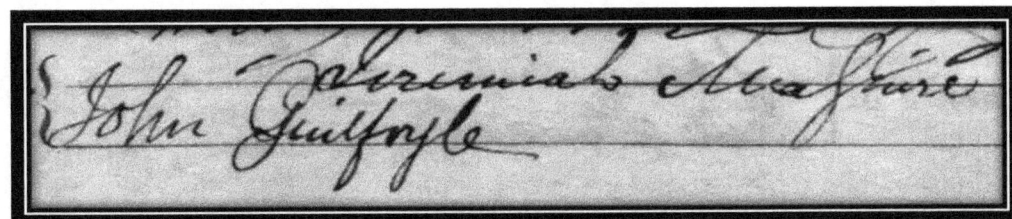

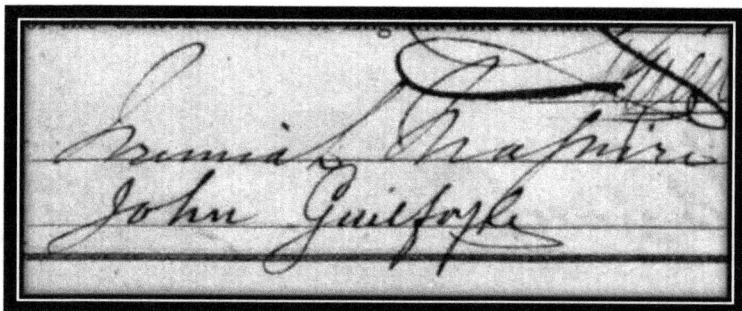

- John Crozier & Unknown

  o Mary Crozier & William Smith – 10 Apr 1861 (Marriage, **St. Peter Parish**)

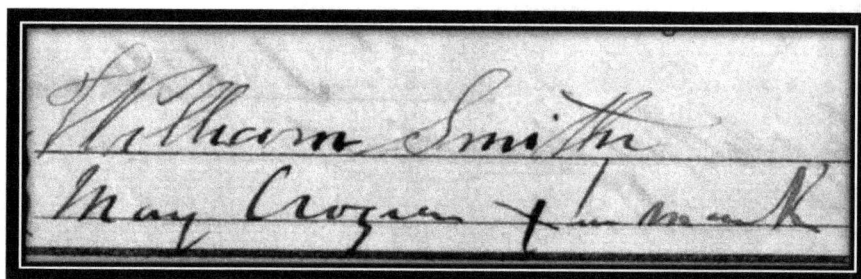

Signatures:

Mary Crozier (daughter):

   Residence - **25** Belgrave Road - April 10, 1861

William Smith, son of William Smith (son-in-law):

   Residence - **25** Belgrave Road - April 10, 1861

   Occupation - Servant - April 10, 1861

   Relationship Status at Marriage - widow

William Smith (father):

   Occupation - Laborer

Crozier Surname Ireland: 1600s to 1900s

John Crozier (father):

    Occupation - Laborer

Wedding Witnesses:

John Gordon & William Lord

Signatures:

- John Crozier & Unknown
  - Emma Mary Crozier & Richard William Morrow – 17 Apr 1866 (Marriage, **St. Peter Parish**)

Signatures:

Emma Mary Crozier (daughter):

    Residence - 9 Fitzwilliam Square - April 17, 1866

Richard William Morrow, son of George Morrow (son-in-law):

    Residence - 9 Fitzwilliam Square - April 17, 1866

    Occupation - Servant - April 17, 1866

Hurst

George Morrow (father):

Residence - Butler

John Crozier (father):

Occupation - Clerk in the Court of Chancery

Wedding Witnesses:

John Pike & Thomas Wilson

Signatures:

- John Crozier & Unknown
  - Mary Anne Crozier & Samuel Hosford – 6 Oct 1869 (Marriage, **St. Stephen Parish**)

Signatures:

Mary Anne Crozier (daughter):

Residence - 22 Lansdowne Road - October 6, 1869

Samuel Hosford, son of Samuel Hosford (son-in-law):

Residence - Phoenix Park Depot - October 6, 1869

Crozier Surname Ireland: 1600s to 1900s

Occupation - Sub Constable R. I. C. - October 6, 1869

Samuel Hosford (father):

Occupation - Land Steward

John Crozier (father):

Occupation - Drum Major, 95th Regiment

Wedding Witnesses:

Mary Moore & Joseph MacLean

Signatures:

- John Young Crozier & Mary Anne Crozier

   - Martha Elizabeth Crozier – bapt. 26 Nov 1809 (Baptism, **St. Paul Parish**)

- Mervin Crozier & Berisford Adams – 27 Dec 1834 (Marriage, **St. George Parish**)

Signatures:

Mervin Crozier (husband):

Residence - Nelson Street, St. George Parish - December 27, 1834

Occupation - Esquire - December 27, 1834

Hurst

Berisford Adams (wife):

Residence - St. George Parish - December 27, 1834

Wedding Witnesses:

James Adams, Edward Crozier, and William St. George

Signatures:

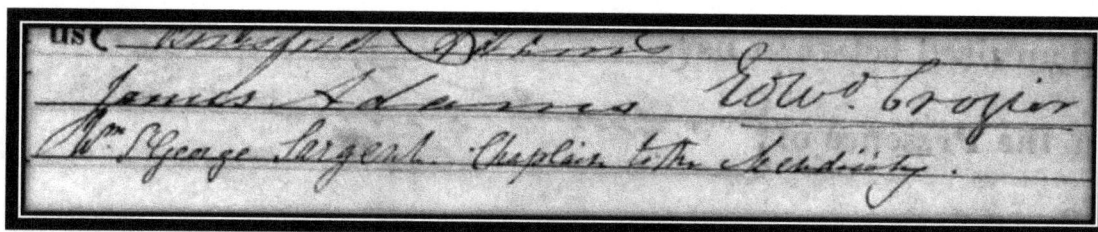

- Philip Crozier & Margaret Unknown

  o Philip Crozier – bapt. 1845 (Baptism, St. Andrew Parish (RC))

- Robert Crozier & Anne Unknown

  o Anne Crozier – bapt. 7 Sep 1790 (Baptism, St. Audoen Parish (RC))

  o Robert Crozier – bapt. 12 Mar 1792 (Baptism, St. Audoen Parish (RC))

  o Andrew Crozier – bapt. 21 Apr 1794 (Baptism, St. Audoen Parish (RC))

  o Bridget Crozier – bapt. 21 Apr 1794 (Baptism, St. Audoen Parish (RC))

Crozier Surname Ireland: 1600s to 1900s

- Samuel Crozier & Unknown
  - James Crozier & Margaret Nugent – 21 Jul 1897 (Marriage, **Rathmines Parish**)

Signatures:

James Crozier (son):

   Residence - Police Barracks, Rathmines - July 21, 1897

   Occupation - Constable D M P - July 21, 1897

Margaret Nugent, daughter of Michael Nugent (daughter-in-law):

   Residence - 94 Rathmines Road - July 21, 1897

Michael Nugent (father):

   Occupation - Sergeant R I C

Samuel Crozier (father):

   Occupation - Farmer

Wedding Witnesses:

Marion Graham & John St. Coleman

Signatures:

Hurst

- Stanley Crozier & Ellen Crozier

  ○ Constance Stanley Crozier – bapt. 27 May 1870 (Baptism, **Arbour Hill Barracks Parish**)

Stanley Crozier (father):

Residence - Royal Barracks - May 27, 1870

Occupation - Captain, 43 Light Infantry - May 27, 1870

- Thomas Crozier & Margaret Crozier

  ○ Mary Anne Crozier & Gulielmo Shaw – 3 Apr 1878 (Marriage, **St. Mary, Pro Cathedral Parish (RC)**)

    ▪ Gulielmo Shaw – b. 24 Aug 1879, bapt. 29 Aug 1879 (Baptism, **St. Agatha Parish (RC)**)

    ▪ Christopher Shaw – b. 15 Dec 1881, bapt. 16 Dec 1881 (Baptism, **St. Agatha Parish (RC)**)

Mary Anne Crozier (daughter):

Residence - 30 Upper Mecklenburgh Street - April 3, 1878

Gulielmo Shaw, son of James Shaw & Anne Shaw (son-in-law):

Residence - 30 Upper Mecklenburgh Street - April 3, 1878

Drumcondra Cottage - August 29, 1879

12 Whitworth Place - December 16, 1881

Wedding Witnesses:

Jane O'Reilly & Bridget Taylor

  ○ Henry Crozier & Roseanne Henry – 3 Dec 1878 (Marriage, **St. Mary, Pro Cathedral Parish (RC)**)

Crozier Surname Ireland: 1600s to 1900s

- Mary Teresa Crozier – b. 15 Oct 1879, bapt. 20 Oct 1879 (Baptism, **St. Michan Parish (RC)**)

- Thomas Henry Crozier – b. 25 Mar 1881, bapt. 28 Mar 1881 (Baptism, **St. Mary, Pro Cathedral Parish (RC)**)

- Roseanne Crozier – b. 8 May 1883, bapt. 16 May 1883 (Baptism, **St. Mary, Pro Cathedral Parish (RC)**)

- Margaret Patrick Crozier, b. 14 Mar 1886, bapt. 19 Mar 1886 (Baptism, **St. Mary, Pro Cathedral Parish (RC)**) & Michael Healy – 15 May 1904 (Marriage, **St. Mary, Pro Cathedral Parish (RC)**)

Margaret Patrick Crozier (daughter):

Residence - 5 Bolton Parade - May 15, 1904

Michael Healy, son of Thomas Healy & Ellen Brennan (son-in-law):

Residence - 4 Bolton Parade - May 15, 1904

Wedding Witnesses:

William Tyrell & Mary Sheiran

- Marcella Crozier – b. 4 Sep 1888, bapt. 7 Sep 1888 (Baptism, **St. Mary, Pro Cathedral Parish (RC)**)

Henry Crozier (son):

Residence - 4 Lower Britain Street - December 3, 1878

12 Mary's Lane - October 20, 1879

7 Green Street - March 28, 1881

May 16, 1883

Hurst

March 19, 1886

September 7, 1888

Roseanne Henry, daughter of John Henry & Rose Unknown (daughter-in-law):

Residence - 4 Lower Britain Street - December 3, 1878

Wedding Witnesses:

Michael Gaffney & Anne Judge

- Thomas Crozier & Mary Crozier
  - George Darley Crozier – b. 7 Oct 1824, bapt. 7 Nov 1824 (Baptism, **St. Mary Parish**)
  - Thomas Francis Crozier – b. 24 May 1826, bapt. 22 Jun 1826 (Baptism, **St. Mary Parish**)
  - Echlin Matthews Crozier – b. 12 Sep 1827, bapt. 23 Sep 1827 (Baptism, **St. Mary Parish**)
  - Amelia Darley Crozier, bapt. 20 Feb 1829 (Baptism, **St. Mary Parish**) & Henry Malkin Barton – 6 Jun 1865 (Marriage, **Taney Parish**)

Amelia Darley Crozier (daughter):

Residence - Seafield - June 6, 1865

Henry Malkin Barton, son of John Barton (son-in-law):

Residence - Stone House, Donnybrook - June 6, 1865

Occupation - Notary, etc. - June 5, 1865

John Barton (father):

Occupation - Gentleman

Thomas Crozier (father):

Occupation - Solicitor

Crozier Surname Ireland: 1600s to 1900s

Wedding Witnesses:

Thomas Francis Crozier & Francis Rawdon Moira Crozier

- o   Graham Philip Crozier – bapt. 14 May 1832 (Baptism, **St. Mary Parish**), bur. 22 Jan 1834 (Burial,

    St. Mary Parish)

Graham Philip Crozier (son):

Residence - Dominick Street - before January 22, 1834

Age at Death - 2 years

- o   Henry Darley Crozier – b. 31 May 1837, bapt. 8 Jun 1837 (Baptism, **St. George Parish**)
- o   Francis Rawdon Moira Crozier, b. 21 Mar 1839, bapt. 13 Apr 1839 (Baptism, **St. George Parish**) &

    Catherine Sophie Mary Manden

    - ▪ Kathleen Amelia Crozier – b. 28 Oct 1870, bapt. 23 Dec 1870 (Baptism, **St. Mary Parish**)
    - ▪ Thomas Francis Crozier – b. 1872, bapt. 1873 (Baptism, **Sandford Parish**)
    - ▪ William Mayne Crozier – b. 5 Dec 1873, bapt. 22 Mar 1874 (Baptism, **Taney Parish**)
    - ▪ George Crozier – b. 1875, bapt. 1875 (Baptism, **Sandford Parish**)
    - ▪ Louis Herbert Crozier – b. 29 Dec 1877, bapt. 20 Apr 1878 (Baptism, **Taney Parish**)

Francis Rawdon Moira Crozier (son):

Residence - 19 Lower Dominick Street - December 23, 1870

15 Aylesbury Road - 1873

Seafield - March 22, 1874

St. Bridget, Clonskea - 1875

Roebuck House - April 20, 1878

Hurst

Occupation - Solicitor - December 23, 1870

1873

1875

Gentleman - March 22, 1874

April 20, 1878

Thomas Crozier (father):

Residence - Dominick Street - June 22, 1826

September 23, 1827

3 Dominick Street - February 20, 1829

May 14, 1832

No. 2 Rutland Square - June 8, 1837

April 13, 1839

Occupation - Solicitor - February 20, 1829

May 14, 1832

April 13, 1839

Esquire - June 8, 1837

- Thomas Crozier & Unknown
  - Jane Elliot Crozier & George Campbell Williams – 5 Dec 1877 (Marriage, **Taney Parish**)

Jane Elliott Crozier (daughter):

Residence - 8 St. James Terrace, Clonskeagh - December 5, 1877

Crozier Surname Ireland: 1600s to 1900s

George Campbell Williams, son of George Campbell Williams (son-in-law):

    Residence - Curragh Camp, Co. Kildare - December 5, 1877

    Occupation - Clerk in Holy Orders - December 5, 1877

George Campbell Williams (father):

    Occupation - Solicitor

Thomas Crozier (father):

    Occupation - Solicitor

Wedding Witnesses:

Frances Naher Davis & Henry D. Crozier

- Unknown Crozier & Jane Magee (1st Marriage)
- Jane Magee Crozier (2nd Marriage) & Francis Clarke – 11 Apr 1860 (Marriage, **Taney Parish**)

Jane Magee Crozier, daughter of Charles Magee (wife):

    Residence - Bellevue - April 11, 1860

Francis Clarke, son of Richard Clarke (husband):

    Residence - Sydney Avenue, Blackrock - April 11, 1860

    Occupation - Medical Doctor - April 11, 1860

Richard Clarke (father):

    Occupation - Clerk

Charles Magee (father):

    Occupation - Esquire, J. P. [Justice of Peace]

Hurst

Wedding Witnesses:

George Crozier & Jonathan Clarke

- Unknown Crozier & Martha Crozier

  - Robert Scott Crozier – b. 12 Apr 1893, bapt. 18 Oct 1893 (Baptism, **St. Mark Parish**)

Martha Crozier (mother):

Residence - 22 Lower Erne Street - October 18, 1893

- Unknown Crozier & Unknown

  - E. F. Crozier

Signatures:

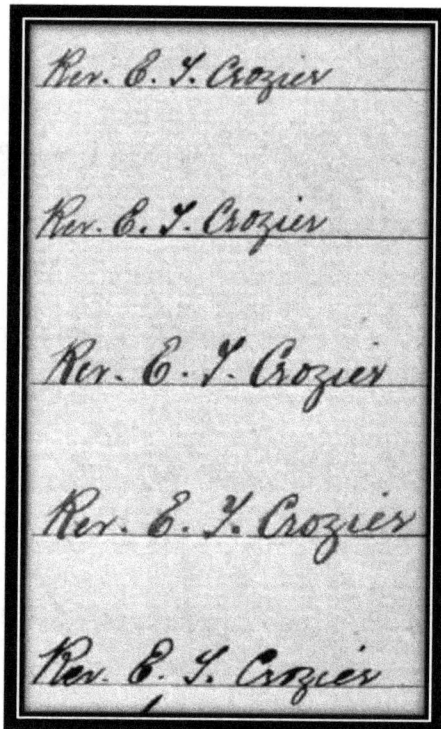

Crozier Surname Ireland: 1600s to 1900s

E. F. Crozier (son):

Occupation - Reverend

- Unknown Crozier & Unknown

  o Edward F. Crozier

Signature:

- Unknown Crozier & Unknown

  o James Crozier

Signature:

- Unknown Crozier & Unknown

  o James Crozier

Signature:

- Unknown Crozier & Unknown

  o John Crozier

Signature:

- Unknown Crozier & Unknown

  o John William Crozier

Signature:

- William Crozier & Hannah Holland – 10 Unclear [Page indicating the month is missing] 1855 (Marriage, **St. Mary, Pro Cathedral Parish (RC)**)

- William Crozier & Martha Unknown

  o Henry Crozier – bapt. May 1846 (baptism, **SS. Michael & John Parish (RC)**)

- William Crozier & Unknown

  o Graham F. Crozier – bur. 26 May 1828 (Burial, **St. Mary Parish**)

Graham F. Crozier (son):

Residence - Blessington Street - before May 26, 1828

William Crozier (father):

Residence - Blessington Street - May 26, 1828

Crozier Surname Ireland: 1600s to 1900s

- William Crozier & Unknown

  - George Crozier & Emily Anne Foster McClintock – 9 Jul 1857 (Marriage, **St. George Parish**)

Signatures:

George Crozier (son):

    Residence - 24 Middle Gardiner Street - July 9, 1857

    Occupation - Solicitor - July 9, 1857

Emily Anne Foster McClintock, daughter of Henry McClintock (daughter-in-law):

    Residence - 9 Upper Gardiner Street - July 9, 1857

Henry McClintock (father):

    Occupation - Esquire

William Crozier (father):

    Occupation - Esquire

Wedding Witnesses:

Edward St. Dix & William Crozier

Signatures:

Hurst

- William Crozier & Unknown

  - James Frederick William Crozier & Sarah Louisa Molony – 28 Aug 1873 (Baptism, **St. Paul Parish**)

Signatures:

Signatures (Marriage):

- John James Crozier – b. 17 Sep 1874, bapt. 1 Nov 1874 (Baptism, **St. Paul Parish**)

- James Frederick William Crozier – b. 30 Aug 1876, bapt. 22 Oct 1876 (Baptism, **St. James Parish**)

Signature:

- Edith Mary Crozier – b. 22 Sep 1878, bapt. 8 Dec 1878 (Baptism, **St. James Parish**)

- Herbert Charles Crozier – b. 3 Jan 1881, bapt. 27 Mar 1881 (Baptism, **St. Paul Parish**)

Crozier Surname Ireland: 1600s to 1900s

- Beatrice Sarah Marian Crozier – b. 14 Nov 1884, bapt. 14 Dec 1884 (Baptism, **St. Paul Parish**)

- Gerard Irvine Crozier – b. 5 Aug 1886, bapt. 12 Sep 1886 (Baptism, **St. Paul Parish**)

- Irene Victoria Crozier – b. 11 Jan 1888, bapt. 1 Apr 1888 (Baptism, **St. Paul Parish**)

James Frederick William Crozier (son):

Residence - Constabulary Depot - August 28, 1873

Constabulary Depot Phoenix Park - November 1, 1874

Royal Constabulary Depot - October 22, 1876

R. I. C. Depot - December 8, 1878

36 Park Gate - March 27, 1881

1 Montpelier Hill - December 14, 1884

September 12, 1886

April 1, 1888

Occupation - Farrier, Sergeant R. I. C. - August 28, 1873

Farrier Sergeant - November 1, 1874

October 22, 1876

December 8, 1878

R. I. C. - March 1, 1881

Veterinary Surgeon - December 14, 1884

September 12, 1886

April 1, 1888

Hurst

Sarah Louisa Molony, daughter of John Thomas Molony (daughter-in-law):

Residence - 2 Park Gate - August 28, 1873

Relationship Status at Marriage - minor

John Thomas Molony (father):

Signature:

Occupation - Merchant

William Crozier (father):

Occupation - Farmer

Wedding Witnesses:

John Thomas Molony & Hester Grealey

Signatures:

Crozier Surname Ireland: 1600s to 1900s

- William Crozier & Unknown

  - Jane Crozier & Robert Little – 24 Nov 1873 (Marriage, **St. Stephen Parish**)

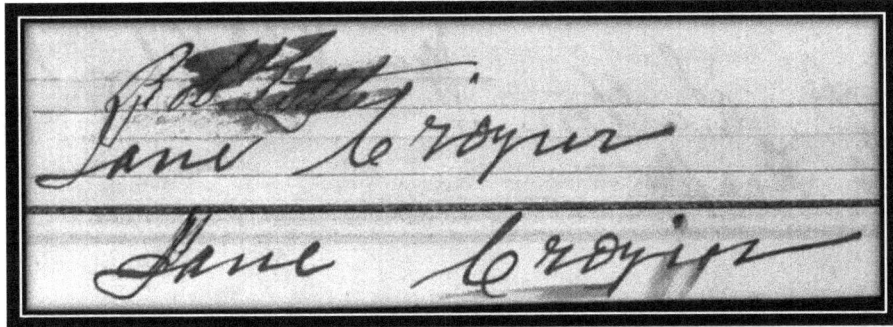

Signatures:

Jane Crozier (daughter):

   Residence - 46 Lower Mount Street - November 24, 1873

Robert Little, son of Isaac Little (son-in-law):

   Residence - Farm Hill Clony, Co. Monaghan - November 24, 1873

   Occupation - Farmer - November 24, 1873

   Relationship Status at Marriage - widow

Isaac Little (father):

   Occupation - Farmer

William Crozier (father):

   Occupation - Farmer

Hurst

Wedding Witnesses:

James Garland & Jane Gray

Signatures:

* William Crozier & Unknown
  * Mary Jane Crozier & Robert Adamson – 6 Jan 1899 (Marriage, **North Strand Parish**)

Signatures:

Mary Jane Crozier (daughter):

Residence - 44 Spring Garden Street, Drumreilly, Co. Lutrum - January 6, 1899

Robert Adamson, son of Robert Adamson (son-in-law):

Residence - Liffey Junction, Cabra - January 6, 1899

Occupation - Railway Foreman - January 6, 1899

Relationship Status at Marriage - widow

Crozier Surname Ireland: 1600s to 1900s

Robert Adamson (father):

    Occupation - Farmer

William Crozier (father):

    Occupation - Farmer

Wedding Witnesses:

Thomas Dickson & John Crozier

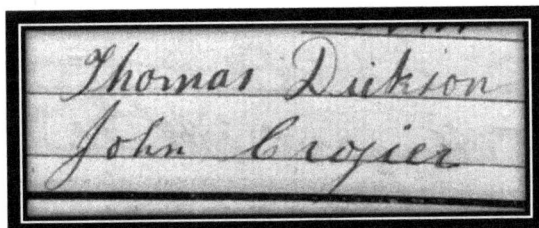

Signatures:

- William John Crozier & Catherine Unknown
    - Catherine Crozier – bapt. 21 May 1821 (Baptism, **St. Mary, Pro Cathedral Parish (RC)**)
    - Margaret Crozier – bapt. Sep 1822 (Baptism, **St. Mary, Pro Cathedral Parish (RC)**)
    - William Crozier – bapt. 5 Aug 1824 (Baptism, **St. Mary, Pro Cathedral Parish (RC)**)
    - Elizabeth Crozier – bapt. 7 Nov 1827 (Baptism, **St. Mary, Pro Cathedral Parish (RC)**)

William John Crozier (father):

    Residence - Lower Liffy Street - May 21, 1821

        Liffy Street - September 1822

            November 7, 1827

Individual Baptisms/Births

None were Listed

Individual Burials

- James Crozier – b. 1795, bur. 29 Sep 1844 (Burial, **St. Mary Parish**)

James Crozier (deceased):

   Residence - Britain Street - before September 29, 1844

   Age at Death - 49 years

- John Crozier – bur. 21 Jan 1816 (Burial, **St. Mary Parish**)

John Crozier (deceased):

   Residence - Britain Street - before January 21, 1816

- John George Crozier – b. 1842, bur. May 1847 (Burial, **St. Nicholas Without Parish**)

John George Crozier (deceased):

   Residence - Kevin Street - before May 1847

   Age at Death - 5 years

- Margaret Crozier – bur. 3 Sep 1747 (Burial, **St. Paul Parish**)

Margaret Crozier (deceased):

   Age at Death - child

Hurst

- Mariah Crozier – bur. 22 Jul 1791 (Burial, **St. Paul Parish**)

- Martha Crozier – b. 1819, bur. 23 Sep 1896 (Burial, **St. George Parish**)

Martha Crozier (deceased):

Residence - 12 Appian Way - September 23, 1896

Age at Death - 77 years

- Mary Crozier – bur. 10 Jul 1791 (Burial, **St. Paul Parish**)

- Mary Crozier – b. 1740, bur. 26 Jun 1836 (Burial, **St. Mary Parish**)

Mary Crozier (deceased):

Residence - 175 Great Britain Street - June 26, 1836

Age at Death - 96 years

- Mary Crozier – b. 1792, d. 22 Feb 1859, bur. 1859 (Burial, **St. James Parish**)

Mary Crozier (deceased):

Residence - St. James Parish - February 22, 1859

Age at Death - 67 years

- Robert Crozier – b. 1815, bur. 10 Jan 1857 (Burial, **St. Nicholas Without Parish**)

Robert Crozier (deceased):

Residence - Ship Street - before January 10, 1857

Age at Death - 42 years

Crozier Surname Ireland: 1600s to 1900s

- Sophie Crozier – b. 1816, bur. 24 Jan 1893 (Burial, St. George Parish)

Sophie Crozier (deceased):

Residence - 12 Appian Way - before January 24, 1893

Age at Death - 77 years

Remarks about Burial - paid on March 22, 1893

Individual Marriages

- Anne Crozier & Thomas Cochran – 15 Dec 1816 (Marriage, **St. Paul Parish**)

- Anne Mary Crozier & John Phelan – 23 Sep 1835 (Marriage, **Tralee Parish**)

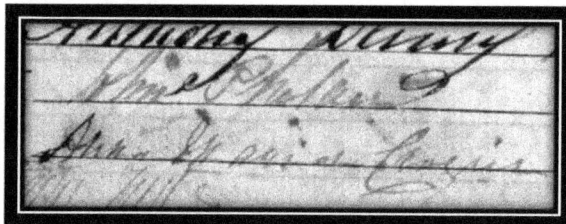

Signatures:

- o Edward John Phelan – b. 8 Jul 1842, bapt. 8 Jul 1842 (Baptism, **Tralee Parish (RC)**)

- o Francis Phelan – b. 8 Jul 1842, bapt. 8 Jul 1842 (Baptism, **Tralee Parish (RC)**)

- o Julie Phelan – b. 6 Feb 1845, bapt. 6 Feb 1845 (Baptism, **Tralee Parish (RC)**)

- o Ellen Phelan – b. 21 Feb 1846, bapt. 21 Feb 1846 (Baptism, **Tralee Parish (RC)**)

John Phelan (father):

Residence - Tralee - July 8, 1842

February 6, 1845

- Bridget Crozier & George Taylor
  - o Thomas Taylor – b. 17 Jul 1872, bapt. 19 Jul 1872 (Baptism, **St. Mary, Pro Cathedral Parish (RC)**)

  - o Henry Taylor – b. 10 Aug 1873, bapt. 11 Aug 1873 (Baptism, **St. Mary, Pro Cathedral Parish (RC)**)

Crozier Surname Ireland: 1600s to 1900s

George Taylor (father):

Residence - 64 Capel Street - July 19, 1872

August 11, 1873

- Bridget Crozier & Thomas Stokes – 27 Oct 1845 (Marriage, **St. Andrew Parish** (RC))

Wedding Witnesses:

Robert Crozier & Anne Corcoran

- Elizabeth Crozier & John Dunne
    - John Ignatius Dunne – b. 4 Sep 1873, bapt. 9 Sep 1873 (Baptism, **St. Audoen Parish** (RC))
    - Mary Emma Dunne – b. 8 Apr 1875, bapt. 12 Apr 1875 (Baptism, **St. Audoen Parish** (RC))
    - Emily Dunne – b. 14 Sep 1876, bapt. 18 Sep 1876 (Baptism, **St. Audoen Parish** (RC))
    - Margaret Mary Dunne – b. 18 Jan 1880, bapt. 23 Jan 1880 (Baptism, **St. Audoen Parish** (RC))

John Dunne (father):

Residence - 6 Oriel Place - September 9, 1873

January 23, 1880

6 Hill Place - April 12, 1875

6 Britt Place - September 18, 1876

- Elizabeth Crozier & John Hollywood
    - Alexander Joseph Hollywood & Mary Josephine Crowe – 3 Jul 1901 (Marriage, **St. Mary, Pro Cathedral Parish** (RC))

Hurst

Alexander Joseph Hollywood (son):

    Residence - 44 Belvidere Place - July 3, 1901

Mary Josephine Crowe, daughter of Dennis Crowe & Mary Anne Hunt

(daughter-in-law):

    Residence - 44 Belvidere Place - July 3, 1901

Wedding Witnesses:

Patrick Chadwick & Mary Josephine Fogarty

- Elizabeth Crozier & Patrick John Malone – 7 Nov 1802 (Marriage, **St. Mary Parish**)
  - Sarah Malone – bapt. 6 Nov 1803 (Baptism, **St. Michan Parish (RC)**)
  - Mary Malone – bapt. 10 Jan 1805 (Baptism, **St. Michan Parish (RC)**)
  - Elizabeth Malone – bapt. 9 Feb 1806 (Baptism, **St. Michan Parish (RC)**)
  - John Malone – bapt. 10 Feb 1808 (Baptism, **St. Michan Parish (RC)**)
  - Simon Michael Malone – bapt. 29 Sep 1816 (Baptism, **St. Michan Parish (RC)**)
  - Francis Malone – bapt. 3 Oct 1819 (Baptism, **St. Michan Parish (RC)**)
- Emma Crozier & Gulielmo Morrow
  - Emma Morrow – bapt. 4 Nov 1872 (Baptism, **St. Mary, Donnybrook Parish (RC)**)

Gulielmo Morrow (father):

    Residence - Donnybrook - November 4, 1872

- Hannah Crozier & Samuel Law – 9 Jul 1788 (Marriage, **St. Paul Parish**)

Crozier Surname Ireland: 1600s to 1900s

- Margaret Crozier & George Sparling – 22 Feb 1835 (Marriage, **St. Audoen Parish**)

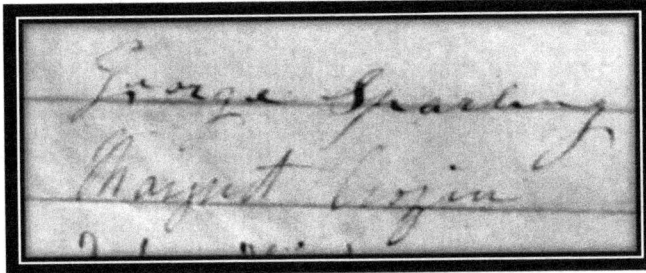

Signatures:

Margaret Crozier (wife):

    Residence - High Street - February 22, 1835

George Sparling (husband):

    Residence - High Street - February 22, 1835

Wedding Witnesses:

John Fisher & Richard McGill

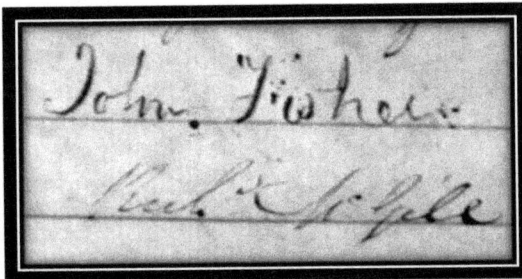

Signatures:

- Margaret Crozier & John Kohan – 12 Jul 1853 (Baptism, **Courcy's Country or Ballinspittal Parish (RC)**)

- Mary Crozier & Patrick Sugrue
  - Cornelius (C o r n e l i u s) Sugrue – bapt. May 1849 (Baptism, **Bantry Parish (RC)**)

Hurst

- Mary Anne Crozier & Patrick Smyth

  o William Smyth & Frances Kavanagh – 29 Jun 1892 (Marriage, **St. Mary, Donnybrook Parish (RC)**)

William Smyth (son):

Residence - 44 Temple Road, Blackrock - June 29, 1892

Frances Kavanagh, daughter of William Kavanagh & Mary Davis (daughter-in-law):

Residence - 12 St. James Terrace, Donnybrook - June 29, 1892

Wedding Witnesses:

James Griffin & Anne Kavanagh

- Mary Jane Crozier & William Jones – 2 Sep 1854 (Marriage, **St. Mary, Pro Cathedral Parish (RC)**)

Wedding Witnesses:

John Teenen & Anne Crozier

Crozier Surname Ireland: 1600s to 1900s

Name Variations

Includes Latin and Abbreviated forms of names found in the original documents.

Abigail = Abigale, Abigall

Anne = Ann, Anna, Annae

Bartholomew = Barth, Bartholmeus, Bartholomeo

Bridget = Birgis, Brigid, Brigida, Bridgit

Catherine = Catharine, Catharina, Catharinae, Catherina, Cath, Catha, Cathae, Cathe, Cathn, Kate

Charles = Carolus, Charls, Chas

Christopher = Christoph

Daniel = Danielem, Danielis

Edmund = Edmond

Edward = Ed, Edwd

Eleanor = Eleo, Eleonora, Elinor, Ellenor

Elizabeth = Betty, Elisa, Elisabeth, Eliz, Eliza, Elizab, Elizh, Elizth

Ellen = Elena, Ellena

Emily = Emilia

Esther = Essie, Ester

Francis = Fransicum

George = Geo, Georg, Georgius

Grace = Gratiae

Gulielmo = Guil, Guillelmi, Gulielmum, Guillelmus, Gulmi

Helen = Helena

Crozier Surname Ireland: 1600s to 1900s

Honor = Hanora, Honora

James = Jacobi, Jacobus, Jas

Jane = Joanna

Jeanne = Jeannae, Joannae

Joan = Johanna, Joney

John = Jno, Joannem, Joannes, Johannis

Joseph = Jos

Juliana = Julian

Leticia = Letitia, Lettice, Letticia

Lewis = Louis

Luke = Lucas

Margaret = Margarita, Margaritae, Margeret, Marget, Margt

Martha = Marthae

Mary = Maria, My

Mary Anne = Marianna, Marianne, Maryanne

Michael = Michaelis, Michl

Patrick = Pat, Patt, Patk, Patricii, Patricius

Peter = Petri

Richard = Ricardi, Ricardus, Rich, Richd

Robert = Roberti

Rose = Rosa, Rosae

Thomas = Thom, Thomae, Thoms, Thos, Ths

Timothy = Timotheus, Timy

William = Wil, Will, Willm, Wm

Notes

Notes

Notes

Notes

Notes

Notes

Index

Hurst

Crozier Surname Ireland: 1600s to 1900s

Hurst

Hurst

F

H

J

K

L

Crozier Surname Ireland: 1600s to 1900s

Hurst

Whitley

About The Author

Donovan Hurst graduated from San Diego State University with a Bachelor of Arts in the major field of studies of History and a minor in the field of studies of Anthropology. He is a current member of The General Society of Mayflower Descendants and has been conducting genealogical research for over 10 years tracing back his ancestors to their ancestral homelands in Denmark, England, France, Germany, Ireland, Norway, and Scotland.

www.ingramcontent.com/pod-product-compliance
Lightning Source LLC
Chambersburg PA
CBHW080054280326
41934CB00014B/3311